The Politics of Project Management

or

I Know More about This Project Than My Boss

LeRoy C. Davis II

Copyright © 2019 LeRoy C. Davis II
All rights reserved.
ISBN: 9781086005448

DEDICATION

This book is dedicated to all of the young engineers who are just beginning their first major project – and to the many more who wish to learn from their mistakes.

CONTENTS

	Preface	4
1	Choosing to Be A Project Manager	8
2	Embarking On A Career	11
3	Close Encounters of the First Time	16
4	Accepting Politics	19
5	Learning to Walk	24
6	Learning to Talk	29
7	Now I Can Be Heard	31
8	Learning and Practicing Your Profession	38
9	Developing Your Persona	42
10	Learning To Inspire	45
11	Learning To Use People	50
12	Developing Teamwork With An Attitude	53
13	Learning To Be A Spearcatcher	56
14	Still Alive and Ready to Move On	60
15	Understanding Big Business Politics	64
16	Preparing Your Team	68
17	Doing It Your Way	73
18	Expert With An Attitude	78
19	Choose Your Assignments	83
20	Conclusions and Other Thoughts	87

ACKNOWLEDGMENTS

This is to acknowledge all the dedicated bosses, engineers, and clerks who thought enough to help me in my quest to overcome company politics.

A very special thanks to Sandy Morgan and her network of secretaries who helped me manage Union Carbide's extensive political nightmare.

I am particularly grateful to my daughter, Patricia Davis-Muffett, who, although a busy executive with Amazon, took the time to edit and improve this manuscript and help me reach my goal.

I would also like to thank my wife, Carolyn Davis, who has always stood by my side and who convinced me to hang in there for another two years to reach full retirement.

PREFACE

I am writing this book because it needs to be written. Unfortunately, no one who still wants to work can write it. The subtitle, *"I know more about this project than my boss,"* gives you a hint about why that's the case: after writing this book, you'd have to retire or consult. Luckily, I'm retired. So here we go!

In the early 1960's, I read a book called *Up the Organization*, which played a major role in my point of view on company politics. The book's core tenet was the idea that honest, hard work, common sense and the bottom line mean a lot to upper management. One suggestion in the book suggests that if you think you are worth more than you are being paid and your boss is unwilling to give you a raise, you should propose the following: Explain to your boss why you are worth more money and that you are willing to quit and reapply for your job at the increased salary, and with your knowledge and experience, he most certainly would hire you back at the increased salary.[1] Nice theory, but in reality, your boss would probably let you quit and reapply, but wouldn't hire you back because he would probably think you're crazy.

As a young engineer working at the chemical company (Rohm and Haas, in Bristol, Pennsylvania), I didn't know this,

---

[1] Townsend, Robert C. *Up the Organization; How to Stop the Corporation from Stifling People and Strangling Profits*, 1970.

so I decided to apply the theory. My boss at the time was an ex-project management named Donald Ney. I was fortunate that he already knew a lot about politics and also had a great sense of humor. He told me that I didn't have to quit and reapply for my job because he was willing to give me the raise. He also told me that the raise had nothing to do with hard work, common sense or the bottom line. He was giving me the raise because I had the guts to walk into his office and pull such a stupid stunt. I didn't realize it at the time, but that was when I started to understand company politics.

Transactional analysis was a popular subject in project management courses in the '60s. These were "soft skills" classes to help project managers gain the skills they needed to effectively manage project teams. It also helped you to handle the talkative passenger next to you on the plane when you wanted to sleep. These courses helped me to understand how skills develop through phases, and that's why I have decided to organize this book along the phases of maturity: the child, the parent, and the mature adult.

When you began your journey, you don't even know what you don't know about politics. As a result, the "child" phase is marked by luck—and the occasional helping hand from a mature adult who takes an interest in your career. The second phase, the "parent," is marked by a dawning realization that there are politics involved in your job. In this phase, you're less likely to make the same mistakes you made when you were a mere child. Finally, as a "mature adult," you can look back on your career and vow never to make those political mistakes again. Unfortunately, you may actually forget some of those lessons you learned over decades and make mistakes again — even as a mature adult. Hopefully, this book will help you to minimize those mistakes. It's tough to even know when you've reached that final phase, but you do know it when you see it — and one of my mentors and friends, Mr. Robert Kimmons, the acknowledged project management expert, definitely qualifies. I have drawn on many of his insights as I wrote this book and for that, I am very thankful.

One of the other people who motivated me to write this book was a young civil engineer named Sam who worked for me. I had an open door policy while he was working for me, allowing anyone to come to me with questions or problems. Though Sam held a master's degree in project management, he had a lot of questions. It got so bad at one point, that when I heard someone come into my office and had my back to the door, I began just saying, "Hi Sam, is there something I can help you with?" and I was rarely wrong. Looking at Sam was like looking into a mirror. I saw myself in my early career. Really, the problem had little to do with Sam and more to do with the raging politics in our organization. They were the worst I had seen in my 35 years of project management.

I wanted to do something not to just guide Sam, but to help all of the other Sams out there. And that's when I realized the reason there wasn't a book to help these kids because most of the mature adults out there still wanted to work. It's said that the mark of a gentleman is that he can deliver criticism and the person receiving it will thank him for the compliment.

In this book, I will walk you through the three phases of the project management political life cycle, and if you pay close attention, this will help you to avoid some political pitfalls. You'll notice that I'm not promising that you can avoid them all — and you wouldn't want to, because some lessons have to be learned firsthand. Still, my hope is that after reading this book, you'll be able to have a tough conversation with your boss and he'll thank you for the compliment.

1: CHOOSING TO BE A PROJECT MANAGER

A project manager was once described to me as the conductor of an orchestra where all of the musicians are members of different unions. So what would make someone choose this career?

I was fortunate to begin my career with a company that had a career path program. As a degreed mechanical engineer, I rotated through several departments for six months each: Vessel Design (before computers), Utility Equipment Design (refrigeration machines, turbines, etc.), Piping Design, and Project Engineering/Project Management.

At the end of two years, I was called into the Director of Engineering's office to discuss my future. With no idea of the soft skills and politics involved, I made my choice: Project Engineering. During my six-month rotation, I noticed that Project Engineers were always in the center of things, always being asked to solve problems, organize meetings, and especially being asked to meet with the Director of Project Engineering on a regular basis. It all seemed very glamorous. I didn't find out until much later that what went on in those meetings with the Director was far from glamorous. I came into my first assignment at the tail end of detailed design. The bulk of the project team was scheduled to relocate to Houston, Texas, when the design was completed. I was scheduled to clean up the last minute items, facilitate final changes and get the revised prints to the field. Sounds challenging and exciting, right? I was the Project Gofer.

Still, it was my first big assignment and I was feeling pretty proud of myself. I have to admit, I got a little caught up in my own importance. During this time, I was invited to attend a bachelor party for one of the most well liked engineers in the department. It was at the local Elks Lodge, and the drinks were cheap. We were all instructed to be prepared to get up and say something nice (or not so nice) about the groom—depending on how well you knew him. When I got there, most of the young engineers were drinking beer, Mateus or Cold Duck, while the older guys were drinking scotch or martinis. When I walked in, the groom-to-be offered to buy me a martini and I accepted. I had another three or four, eating very little. When the roast began, everyone stood up, told a story or two, and sat down. Then came my turn. Unfortunately, I didn't limit my comments to the groom. I commented on everything I thought was wrong with the engineering division.

The next morning, I was summoned to the Director's office promptly at 8 am. He gave me a couple of early lessons in politics: "It's a bad idea to drink and talk business" and "You shouldn't comment on things you know little about." Then, the conversation turned to my future. I was being assigned temporarily to Houston. It seemed there was an urgent need for a project engineer to take charge of the pipe testing crew, the painting contract, and the insulation contract.

From office gofer to field gofer in five martinis or less. The boss made it sound like this was a good career move, and it was not until many years later that I put the facts together and realized my political mistake. Looking back, that experience was both eye-opening and educational.

When I chose my career, there were few facts at my disposal—especially on the topic of politics. Today, there are both undergraduate and graduate programs in project management at prominent colleges and universities. Still, it seems that politics are rarely mentioned. I had to acquire experience the hard way. Here's hoping the information in this book can be of use to the next generation of project managers.

Early in my career, I heard about a retirement party for one of the senior project managers. Confused about the level of excitement, I asked, "Why the big fuss?" It turned out that this was the first project manager to retire in the history of Corporate Engineering. The rest had died on the job. Still, I don't regret my choice of career. Each day brings new challenges—and it's more fun now that I understand the politics.

2: EMBARKING ON A CAREER

So, my career at Rohm and Haas began on this Houston project. I was assigned as the gofer for an experienced Engineering Aide, Tom Smith. This was before my blunder and I was working out of headquarters in Pennsylvania. I was given specification sheets for equipment, asked to write the requisitions, and send to purchasing for bidding. I was also asked to assemble standards for labor contracts from our files—paper files, since this was pre-computers. Still, I attacked these tasks with the same zeal I employ in my work today.

Mr. Smith, a true gentleman, recognized my enthusiasm, praised me for my work ethic, and encouraged me to think and question everything. He was initialing all of my work and forwarding it to our project manager for authorization. Here is where the politics began to surface.

Mr. Smith went on vacation for a week and left me in charge of getting the work out in his absence. On a very large project, this amounts to a lot of paper, especially near the end of detail design. Every day, I wrote the requisitions, compiled the specifications, and put them on the project manager's desk for his signature and forwarding to purchasing. Now, Mr. Smith hadn't trained me to follow up and see that the requisitions were actually going out. On Monday, he returned to find my weeks' worth of work sitting on his desk for review and approval. This meant the project manager hadn't signed them and apparently didn't trust me to do my job.

Needless to say, Mr. Smith was furious. He called me into his office and instructed me to follow his lead. He was not upset with me, but he wanted to make a point. A few minutes later, he came to the doorway of my office and pretended to be extremely upset. In a very loud voice, he questioned why I didn't get the work out. In fact, he was so loud that the project manager heard every word. Finally, the project manager came out of his office and explained that he was the one who held up the work—not me. After that incident, the project manager trusted me to get the work done.

The lesson? If one seasoned veteran has faith in your work, the others will likely fall in line. The project moved along quickly and in no time, everyone had left for the job site except me. Before Mr. Smith left for Houston, he gave me a new title: Project Coordinator. Taking a page from *Up the Organization*, he explained that I was still the junior engineer on the project and I would still get the grunt work. "Since you're the only one left, it will make you sound more important and help you get things done." This was a smart move because titles are so important in Engineering. Of course, this also paved the way for the infamous bachelor party incident.

I was fortunate to have a boss with a sense of humor who remembered what it was like to be my age. He told me to go home and explain to my wife that we were moving to

Houston in five days. A moving company would come on Friday to pick up our stuff. As you can imagine, this news was not well received on the home front. On Friday, we embarked on an adventure, driving to Houston before today's extensive interstate system existed. We arrived in Houston five days later with my wife ready to get on the next plane home.

Things calmed down, though, and my adventure in the world of construction politics began. Construction politics aren't really much different than project management politics with one major exception: the people are a lot less subtle.

I arrived on the job site at 6:30 in the morning to meet the senior project manager. He started off with a very cool welcome and began describing my job. He handed me two massive volumes of standards — one for the insulation and painting and the the other for the pipe testing. His only instruction was, "You will be in charge of the insulation and painting contract and you will be supervising the pipe testing on the mechanical contract. I assume you know what you are doing on these contracts?" I at least knew enough about politics to lie. I thought, "How hard can it be? Paint, insulation and pipe testing. Piece of cake." I answered with an enthusiastic "Definitely!"

I took the standards for pipe testing home with me after the first day and went through the first several chapters to familiarize myself with the procedures. I arrived the next morning full of enthusiasm and knowledge. The project manager greeted me at the door and explained that he was going to take me over to meet my counterpart at Brown and

Root. At this time, project managers actually went into the field and ran the construction operations. He told me that did not expect to see me in the office until lunchtime and then again at quitting time. By the end of the day, I should know my foreman and all of the crew by first name, and I should learn something about their personal lives. This was some of the best advice I ever got, though I didn't fully appreciate it at the time. This project manager would shape my future and mold my professional character more than anyone else. I followed his advice and things went well for about three weeks.

    As the fourth week began, I was summoned to the Brown and Root office. The project manager there explained the importance of a particular set of lines to the schedule — the critical path for completion. I would have to be sure to inspect them properly. I said I would and thanked their project manager, Emil Zerr, who would eventually become the president of Brown and Root. The first test was being conducted with a pressure gauge that was three times the test pressure. Now, you'll recall that I had studied the standards carefully. The standards called for the gauge to be no more than two and a half times the test pressure. Proud of my academic knowledge, I told the crew that they would have to break down the test and replace the gauge. Of course, Mr. Zerr had assured the Rohm and Haas project manager that the test would be completed by five that day.

    When Mr. Zerr learned that I had halted the test, he was furious. Did I fail to mention that this was a fixed price contract? Needless to say, we restarted the test with the gauge in place (3x pressure) and I stayed late to approve it. The project completed on time and under budget and I survived my first encounter in the field with a new appreciation for the common sense I would need to go along with my engineering degree.

If there is one thing that has served me more than anything else in surviving the politics in the course of my career, it's this one: never discount common sense.

3: CLOSE ENCOUNTERS OF THE FIRST KIND

Speaking of common sense, there are a lot of things I have learned from my construction crews. Please keep in mind that the construction job I'm talking about here was pre-OSHA, so safety and following the rules wasn't always a high priority.

Early in my first trip to Houston, I was asked to verify the alignment of the coupling between the pumps and motors, as well as the rotation of the motors. The latter was easy: I just had to touch the electrical leads to the motor and make sure it turned in the direction indicated by the arrow painted there. If it didn't, I would just reverse the leads and record what I had done. The pump alignment was tougher. The millwrights (these are the mechanics) attached two micrometers to the motor side of the pump with the feet resting on the coupling. As they turned the motor, they got eight different readings. The idea was for the millwrights to work on this and call me to check it when they had it aligned within the margin of error (no more than 0.2 out in any direction). I was ecstatic when the first six pumps I checked were all in perfect alignment: eight zeros, 100% perfect.

As I sat and had a cup of coffee with another engineer, I mentioned how well things were going and the perfect readings on the first six pumps. He raised an eyebrow and asked, "Did you notice whether the micrometer was moving as it rotated around the coupling?" I hadn't given that any thought. That's when he explained how easy it was to jam the micrometer so it would always read eight zeros. He advised me to check the micrometer at the same time I checked the pump. Sure enough, the next pump I checked had a jammed micrometer. The millwright foreman suggested we not make a big fuss and just go back and test the first six pumps again. After that, I had trouble getting eight zeros. In fact, I learned that it was pretty rare to get eight zeros.

    Later, we were hydrostatically testing a pipe. You do this by filling the system with water, pumping the pressure to the right amount and waiting an hour to recheck and see if the pressure holds. If it does, you can be pretty certain you don't have any leaks. Sometimes, these plants have pipe systems that cover thousands of feet, marked out on process flow diagrams. After testing, I would check the gauge and walk the line to check for leaks. If I didn't find any, I would approve the system. From the inspector's guide, I learned that water sitting in steel pipe for an hour under the hot sun could expand and cause the pressure to rise, meaning that it had to be bled off several times — and also that some contractors might try to block in the pressure close to the pump and gauge to make it look like there weren't any leaks. To avoid this, I walked the line to the farthest point and asked for the line to be drained so I could be sure there was water in the whole system. Once, I discovered that the contractor was trying to fool me with this trick, but it only happened once because it was such an embarrassment.

So that was common sense I had to achieve by learning how not to be duped. On the lighter side, I gained some much needed common sense in ways that wouldn't be possible today due to OSHA's excellent work rules.

The contractor told me that I needed to inspect the emergency brake on the elevator and that the best way to do this was from the top of the elevator cab while it was falling. I did and later the project manager asked me, "What would have happened if it hadn't worked?"

Along similar lines, I was told by the contractor that I had to inspect the lights at the top of a stack we had just erected that was 150 feet in the air, and in the flight path for Houston's Hobby Airport. This seemed harmless enough, since they were taking me up in a basket attached to the boom of a crane. They took me to the top and, sure enough, the lights were working. I leaned over the side and signaled that everything was ok and they could lower me to the ground. What followed may have been the start of the sport of bungee jumping – except I didn't sign up for the ride! The very experienced crane operator proceeded to free fall the basket toward the ground while I held on for dear life. He stopped the basket about two feet from the ground, where I found that everyone (except me) was laughing hysterically. They had to pry my shaking hands from the handrail. When the project manager heard what had happened, he asked, "Wouldn't it have been easier to check the lights tonight once it got dark?"

4: ACCEPTING POLITICS

Once I returned from my first field assignment as a Project Engineer, I returned from Houston back to Rohm and Haas headquarters in Bristol, Pennsylvania. Like many enthusiastic young engineers, I returned from the field eager to apply what I had learned and ready for my next assignment. This was a time when companies invested in having their own staff of engineers and designers and didn't mind keeping them on overhead while they waited for their next assignment. Still, it was a tough time for an enthusiastic young engineer. I was chomping at the bit!

The Corporate Engineering Group was quite social and I made many lasting friendships through social activities like softball and golf. One of my friends at this time was a project engineer who had recently been assigned to a medium-sized project, scheduled to be built in Houston. The project manager he was working for had a terrible reputation for being very hard on project engineers. My friend (let's call him "Wack" to protect the innocent) was complaining about how much work he had to do in a short amount of time. Over beers one night, I volunteered to help him out. I figured, "Why not? I have all of this new knowledge and nothing to do with it right now."

I showed up in Wack's office the next day and asked what he needed me to do. He said he needed someone to write the specifications for concrete and structural steel. This was right up my alley, since my first project included a lot of this type of work. I typed it up and put it on Wack's desk for review. After reviewing the specification, Wack's only comment was that I should put my name on the front of it instead of his. I know what some of you are thinking: Wack was just covering his bases in case it was badly written. But we were both too innocent to do that at this point; he just thought it was a good piece of work and wanted me to get credit for it. (And let me tell you, when an engineer says, "This is a good piece of work," it amounts to high praise.)

I had been down this road before and tried to explain to Wack that he should leave his name on it to avoid any trouble that might come from having someone so young and inexperienced writing a specification, but he wouldn't hear of it. He changed the title page and submitted the spec for approval to the senior project manager. I went on my merry way and helped Wack write the structural steel specification.

The next day, during our coffee break, I saw Wack and he was crestfallen. I asked him what was wrong and he told me to come to his office. There on the desk was the concrete spec, returned by the senior project manager. On the cover, my name was crossed out and Wack's was written in. I started to say, "I told you so," when he opened it up and said, "Oh, that's minor." As he leafed through it, it looked like someone had been shaving over it with a hangover. Wack was embarrassed and apologetic, especially about the senior project manager's comment that senior project engineers should write their own specifications and not give them to inexperienced engineers to write. I calmly said, "No problem," and took the spec back to fix it. Wack resubmitted it later that day.

Again, at coffee break the next day, I saw Wack. This time, he was all smiles. We went back to his office and sure enough, there was the specification with a note attached: "That's more like it. This was obviously prepared by a senior project engineer."

A few days later, we submitted the structural steel specification and it was accepted with little comment except a similar note about the engineer's obvious experience. This taught me a valuable lesson about the perceptions of senior engineers. They just couldn't see past someone's inexperience to the quality of their work. If you're a junior engineer on a project and you happen to have come across this book, I give you the following advice: Learn to accept it. Work around it. Don't let it upset you. This will help to keep you off of blood pressure medicine later in life! An awful lot of young engineers have gained valuable experience ghostwriting specifications for overworked older engineers!

Really, the most difficult part about dealing with this kind of politics is learning to accept it. You have to learn from the experience and move on. Some may say that this kind of thing doesn't happen today, but I can tell you about an incident that happened just a few years ago that proves it still does.

I previously mentioned a young engineer I met later in my career named George. George had a tough time accepting the politics I've just been discussing. When George had worked for me for about four years, a senior project manager working for another director had to return home due to a family emergency. Since this emergency was expected to last only a short time, I had to supply a temporary project manager. George was between assignments, so I put him in as the temporary project manager on a $200 million project. Of course, I promised management that I would keep a close eye on the job—something I promised, but didn't do because I knew George was up to the challenge.

George jumped in with both feet and moved the project along without missing a beat. It turned out that the family emergency was serious, so the original project manager never returned. George took the project through the appropriation phase and then, it was put on hold, due to the pending merger between Dow Chemical and Union Carbide. After the merger, the project was reactivated and a search began for a project manager. To Dow's credit, they decided it should be run by a Carbide project manager, since the project relied on Carbide's expertise.

Now, I know you are way ahead of me. Surprise, surprise! George wasn't even considered. Youth, enthusiasm and intelligence were again denied due to company politics. The unwritten policies in engineering dictated that anyone under 30 was incapable of managing a $200 million project. Look around, though. Today, many CEOs are under 30!

The real lesson learned here is to accept the politics (at least for now) and focus on getting experience wherever you can. Remember that the objective is to be prepared when you finally get your shot. You will be ready, knowledgeable and willing to accept the assignment—especially with your keen sense of how to manage company and project politics.

5: LEARNING TO WALK

My moment arrived more quickly than I expected due to the boom in the chemical industry in the late '60s and early '70s. Companies were consuming manpower at a tremendous rate due to huge capital programs. The Chief Project Manager for Rohm and Haas called me into his office and explained that he needed a project manager for a small ($3.5 million) project — a modification to the one I worked on in Houston. It was against his better judgment to give it to me, since I was so young, but he was basically out of options. So, with this resounding vote of confidence, I got my first project.

I started selecting my team from those available. It turned out that we had obtained the process from a Japanese company with the intention of improving it. As a result, we had the flow sheets, but no maintenance or operating instructions. We were allowed one trip to Japan (about two weeks, including travel) to speak with their project team and learn about the process. During this time, I became friends with the Japanese project manager and his family.

After returning from Japan, we moved on to detail design work back at headquarters in Bristol, Pennsylvania. We modified an existing plastic scale model, purchased our equipment and bulks and got ourselves ready to move to the jobsite in Texas. Given the booming construction going on, there was a real bottleneck when you needed help from Corporate Engineering functions, like design, electrical, specialists, and control people. As a young project manager, I was at the bottom of the list, but my work still needed to get done. I figured out quickly that one surefire way to get attention for my work was to offer overtime. This worked well to accomplish the task, but it made the other project managers cranky. Word got back to upper management and I got my wrist slapped, but we got the job done on time. This proves the theory that it's better to ask for forgiveness later than to ask for permission first.

With the design and procurement done, we moved to Houston for construction and startup. The project was relatively simple to construct and was tracking for successful completion. At the end of construction, we had a scheduled shutdown that would last eight weeks. After that, we would startup and sell this wonderful new product. Let me step back a minute, though, and tell you a little about the process so you can better understand the politics.

As we prepared for the shutdown, the plant overproduced the product and began storing it in large tanks in order to cover the eight week shutdown and two week startup. In order to be salable, the product had to have a propionate level of 1.0 or lower. Anything higher couldn't be sold. The new process was supposed to bring that level down to 0.8. Without going into a lot of boring details, suffice it to say that this process mixed multiple chemicals together in a reactor to make a single product. When the reaction had peaked, there was an increase in vent gasses from the reactor. At this point, the operator knew to dump the contents into the storage tanks.

We completed the shutdown in eight weeks and moved into startup mode without proper planning (I would figure that out later) and we were lucky to finish in ten days. We were ready to make the new and improved product! Production started at 10 a.m., thus kicking off the worst four weeks of my life.

The batch was completed in two hours and our technicians took a sample to the lab for analysis. While we waited for the results, we noticed several things we couldn't explain. First, during the later part of the process, the reactor was vibrating quite a bit and the steel was actually shaking. We asked our structural engineer to look into this and let us know if we had a problem. Also, the operator complained that the vent gas spike was not as steep as he had seen it previously and he felt uncomfortable about the timing of completion.

Two hours later, the test results were in: the propionates were at 1.6. This was a total disaster. Over the next four weeks, we made many different batches, but the best we ever achieved was 1.3.

We had enough product stored to carry us through 13 weeks, but now we were on a collision course. With each batch that was over 1.0, we continued to store more off-spec material. Our sales force was out selling a product that we couldn't deliver and this was about to become a political nightmare. The worst project is one that is on time, under budget, but doesn't work!

In week 13, I was sitting in the construction office, dejected, when the phone rang. The caller identified himself as the CEO of Rohm and Haas, Mr. Gregory. The conversation that followed was mostly him talking and me listening. As you can imagine from the antics I've already mentioned, I was highly suspicious that this might be a practical joke. In the middle of the call, the plant alarm went off and I asked if I could call him back. He said yes and gave me his number. When I returned to my desk, I checked the number in the company phone book and sure enough, it was Mr. Gregory's number. I called back and he explained how important this project was to the financial health of the company. As we finished the call, he asked, "Is there anything I can do to help you make this startup happen?"

As I sat in my office contemplating my new career as a used car salesman at about 3 a.m., I decided to do the only thing I could think of that we hadn't tried yet. I called my counterpart in Japan. This was not allowed under the contract, so I called him at home. Luckily, I had forged a relationship with him and his family during my two weeks there.

As I explained the situation, he chuckled and explained that the process consumes approximately 99% of the chemical feeds in the batching operation, so there is very little venting. The vibration was caused by the reaction and would reach a peak at the moment when the batch was complete. He explained that the batch would vent only if it was overreacting, which would cause the propionates to go up. They had used a vibration meter on the reactor that would print out in the control room. I thanked him for his help and spent the rest of the early morning hours formulating a plan.

The next morning, I told our control engineer that he needed to order a vibration meter for the reactor with a remote to the control room. I immediately sent out our materials man to purchase a device like a baby monitor so we could listen to the vibration in the control room in the meantime.

Around 10 a.m., we were ready to start the day's batch. Sure enough, we heard the rumbling from the vibration start and reach a peak. At that moment, I ordered the control man to dump the batch. We anxiously waited for the test results and when they came in…we were at 0.6 propionates. This meant we could mix the good batches with the bad and sell it all. No more calls from the CEO.

On my first day back in Pennsylvania, I was told to report to Mr. Gregory's office in Philadelphia at 10 a.m. Needless to say, I didn't sleep well that night; I was sure I was going to be fired. When I arrived, I was ushered into Mr. Gregory's office and he personally congratulated me for doing a great job and handed me a bonus check that amounted to half of my yearly salary.

So the key lessons here are:
- A project that starts successfully is always better than one that doesn't work, no matter what the timeline and budget look like.

- And most importantly, when the CEO offers help, you'd better come up with something special. That is help you probably don't want or need.

6: LEARNING TO TALK

There is a lot to be said for voicing your opinion, but early in your career, it's unlikely that anyone will listen. Sometimes, the worst case scenario, though, is that someone does listen and take you up on your suggestion.

During almost a decade as a project engineer and project manager, I saw that owners did a very poor job of scheduling and planning. (I even published an article on this topic.) On all of my projects, I saw us bring people in to build two-week look-ahead schedules and the like, but they were mostly valuable as doorstops. A good old bar chart worked best and at the end of one of my projects, I wrote a letter to Rohm and Haas management railing about how much money we were spending on overblown planning and scheduling that added no value. This is where "learning to talk" comes in.

In my ninth year, I was again summoned to the chief engineer's office. (Are you starting to see that I had become quite familiar with this office and its occupants?) On his desk, was a folder of everything I had written (good and bad) about planning and scheduling. In my article, I had stated that owners could save $500K per year by doing their own planning and scheduling. He told me that management had decided to take me up on this and they were going to set up an in-house planning and scheduling group, with me at the helm. I would be given a budget of $100K to hire staff, put a system in place and be prepared to schedule a critical $100M project within six months. He told me I had until 2 p.m. the next day to think it over.

I went home and talked with my wife, who thought it was a great idea since it only required 8 hour days and no travel. I was worried, though, about getting away from what I really loved: project management and construction management. The next day, I agreed to take on the job of setting up the group and making it work — but I would only do it for three years. After that, I wanted to go back into the field. I agreed that I would have someone trained and ready to take over by the time I was ready to leave. I asked to have all of this in writing.

He was surprised at my request to have the agreement written down. I explained my reasons. First, if I was doing a poor job, they would move me out in a heartbeat, but if I was doing well, they would resist letting me return to project management. Second (the politically correct reason), was that if the chief engineer was promoted, no one would know about our agreement. He understood my logic and gave me a letter outlining the details, countersigned by personnel.

I took on my new assignment with enthusiasm and zeal. I staffed the group with in-house people who understood what and how our projects were designed and built. I hired purely for skill and one of my best schedulers was a woman. We were ready to schedule the $100M project.

In my meeting with the senior project manager, I laid out everything we had devised. He listened intently to my plans for procurement issues and construction, reviewed my organization chart and listened to my request for his help in getting his people to cooperate. After what seemed like a very long time (but was really less than an hour), he leaned back in his chair and said, "What you just presented is crap. I'm fairly certain none of it will work, but since management wants this system to succeed, I will give you full cooperation from me and my staff." I was flabbergasted. I asked him, "If you don't believe it will work, why are you willing to cooperate?" His reply was brilliant and showed that he was a master of politics.

"Look," he said, "if your system fails and the project is late, I can blame you and your staff. If the system succeeds and the project is on time and everyone likes your systems, I am the one who helped make it work. I can't lose." He had found the path to assure a win for him and one for me (if my system worked), using his astute understanding of company politics.

Another piece of politics I learned was about managing the professional woman on my team at a time when there were very few professional women, especially in construction project management. I had assigned the woman on my team to work on procurement issues. One evening, I walked past her office (I had turned that 8 to 5 job into a 7 to 7 job after all) and noticed that she was sitting at her desk crying. I walked in and asked what was wrong. She said she had spent all day with a particular project engineer and that he had ridiculed her and given her a very hard time all day. When I heard this, I became irate (and a little insensitive) and tried to fire her up by saying, "I didn't hire you to sit in your office and cry. I hired you to be a scheduler." Her response taught me a lot and is something I have kept in mind ever since: "It's after 5 o'clock and I'm crying on my own time. It took twenty years for women to get into these offices and not just in the secretarial desks, so it might take a little more time for me to overcome my emotions. But don't you worry: tomorrow, I will be back at it and no project engineer will get the best of me." They never did and she became one of the best schedulers we ever had.

One final lesson in learning about talk was in understanding the value of talk and a lesson about what management could be capable of. You see, at the end of three years, we were doing quite well in the scheduling and planning group. Just as agreed, I had trained someone to take over the department. I went to see the chief engineer and reminded him of our arrangement. He pointed out that our major project would be completed in just eight months and asked me to stay for one more year. I reluctantly agreed and at the end of that year, I tried again. This time, I got a different answer. I was told that I was too important to transfer back to project management and since I had already spent 13 years with Rohm and Haas, they were pretty sure I wouldn't leave. Personnel told me their hands were tied without approval of the chief engineer.

I vividly remember the response when I confronted him with that letter sealing our agreement: "So I lied. I need you where you are and that's where you will stay.

7: NOW I CAN BE HEARD

Now comes to the hard part: the fine line between being heard and being aggressive. There were times when I crossed that line and came close to being arrogant or too aggressive. Fortunately for me, at that time, I was right and was producing excellent bottom line results.

When I was department head for the scheduling and planning group, management called for a monthly meeting on the $200M project we were working on. We had produced 22 Gantt (bar) chart schedules for the project—one summary and 21 individual area schedules. The meeting was to occur on the first Monday of the month and management wanted the schedules one week in advance. I argued that we should hand out the schedules in the meeting so that I could wait until the last day of the month, gather data, update the schedules and produce something realistic to discuss. Of course, management won and the schedules were produced a week in advance.

This worked out fine during detail design because it is difficult to see real progress during design without asking questions. Sometimes, asking questions makes management look foolish; therefore, they don't ask. When we moved into construction, though, the real problem began to surface. The whole management group would schedule a trip to the job site just before the meeting. In construction, you don't have to ask questions; you can see progress from week to week. Keep in mind: my schedules were producing data 3 days prior to the issue date and then the schedules were not reviewed by the management team until 7 days later. Several months of frustration followed, where everyone thought the schedules were wrong, since they saw more progress than my schedules indicated. My frustration led to one of those incidents that might be considered arrogant.

I was in the process of producing the monthly schedules as requested, when it hit me. Was anyone actually reading these schedules in advance? We were preparing the packages to mail out to everyone (this was before the electronic age) and I caught sight of a rubber stamp I had sitting on my desk that someone had given me in jest. It read, "BULLSHIT." I suddenly had the urge to prove my point, so I stamped schedule number 13 in each package with the stamp—in RED. And yes, folks, I mailed them out.

Two days later, I received a phone call from the director of process engineering: "I must have gotten a working copy of schedule number 13, because my copy is stamped 'bullshit.'" I confessed that I had done that deliberately to see if any of the 15 people in the meting actually read the schedules in advance. I received no more phone calls.

As usual, we gathered on the first Monday of the month to review the schedules, one at a time. When we got to schedule 11, the director of process engineering excused himself because he could hardly contain himself. Well, when we got to schedule 13, there was a great deal of conversation about the stamp. The vice president of engineering angrily questioned why I had done this. I explained that I had to prove a point that couldn't be proven any other way. No one, with the exception of the director of process engineering, had read the schedules before the meeting. Since that was the case, I suggested that they let me produce the schedules later and hand them out at the meeting. All agreed and I was not fired.

After the meeting, I was called into the vice president's office. He told me that he didn't mind what I had done, but he did ask that if I was going to do something like this in the future, please let him in on it beforehand. It isn't nice to embarrass vice presidents — even when you are right. Being heard and listened to does come with some responsibilities.

The next incident occurred while I was working for BASF in Parsippany, New Jersey. I was the project manager for a new indigo dye plant. My team and I had worked on the project for about a year and had developed a planning model with a scope to prepare a 10% estimate. The corporate engineering group in Germany decided to send a group of engineers to review the estimate. We had two weeks' advance notice for the weeklong meetings. I set up a dress rehearsal a week before and my boss (who had come to the company through an acquisition of Wyandotte Chemical) cleared his schedule to participate. We felt pretty confident about our strategy for the meeting and our position on all of the subjects that were likely to come up. The one area we weren't prepared well for was the Sodium Unloading area, but we thought we could gloss over these issues with our German counterparts. Everyone agreed and we proceeded with the meetings with this strategy in place.

Our German colleagues arrived and we spent five days poring over the details of the project—everything except the Sodium Unloading, which we had successfully skirted by stating that we were going to match Dupont's facility in Wilmington. We failed to mention that we didn't have that information and were only guessing on its cost.

During the Friday wrap-up meeting, the lead engineer from Germany was making a summary speech and complimenting us on how good our presentation was and how thorough we had been in putting together the estimate. Then, he directed a question to my boss: "What questions have we failed to ask?" To everyone's astonishment, he replied: "You really didn't ask much about the Sodium Unloading and that's our weakest area." The project was delayed and eventually cancelled, in part due to this comment.

The real political moment here came in the meeting that immediately followed this comment. My boss called me into his office to inquire about how he had done in the meeting. Everything I had learned about politics was obliterated by the emotion of the moment and I said, "Do you want the answer that will affect my raise or do you want the truth?" His answer: "Give me the one that affects your raise." So I said,

"You did terrific."

This was the perfect example of George Bernard Shaw's definition of a true English gentleman ("a man who never gives offence unintentionally"). Really, I should have stopped and thought of the right words to properly insult him. I was amazed when he dismissed me without a comment, thinking I was home free. The following Monday morning, though, he appeared in my office and told me that he did not appreciate my insult in our previous conversation. And really, in this situation, my insult didn't improve the situation; the damage was already done. All I did was make things harder for myself.

So, in summary, while it's important to be heard, you have to consider your audience and temper what you say depending on who is doing the asking. For instance, if a vice president asks for your opinion on a project, it might be useful to understand where he stands before you make your opinion know. You might respond with, "I don't have enough information yet, but I'd like your input as I'm gathering data.

Speaking the truth, while important, is not always the wise thing to do. Don't lie, but sometimes you may want to withhold your opinion and find a better time or manner to get your voice heard.

8: LEARNING AND PRACTICING YOUR PROFESSION

The first section of this book covered the Formative Years—and during my formative years, I was lucky to work for Rohm and Haas, a company that was more interested in developing strong project managers than punishing project engineers who make innocent political mistakes (like truthfully answering the question, "What do you think of this project?"). If you're reading this book and working somewhere that punishes your mistakes instead of helping you grow, finish reading and then go apply for a job at a more progressive company.

This next section deals with the middle years of your career, where you move from "child" to "parent." In this phase of your project management career, you begin to apply some of the lessons learned in the formative years and add some reality to your judgement. You now know that stepping into the phone booth and changing into that suit with the big S on the front will no longer suffice. As adults, we begin to temper our judgement, changing "Anything is Possible" for "Anything is Possible, but…"

During this next phase, you have more freedom in your decision-making if you are working for a progressive company. While working at BASF, I had the opportunity to work for a manager of project engineering who worked hard to develop his people. Rod (as I'll call him) called me into his office one day and told me I would be managing the Indigo Project. He gave me a list of available personnel to interview and told me to make my selections. I did and brought my list to Rod. He responded: "Excellent. I'll try to make this happen." He did and it made me feel important and valued.

Later, I learned from Rod that he liked to let project managers choose their own teams because they would work twice as hard to make the team work if they chose everyone themselves. Otherwise, they were likely to come back to him and ask for people to be replaced. In later years, while working for Union Carbide, I was in a meeting to select the team for a $100M project. The project manager was already selected and he was a true "A" player in his forties with over twenty years of experience. He was a strong, dynamic project manager, so I suggested that we let him select his own team. I explained the political benefits to us and the opportunity to build up this key player. The answer shocked me and helped me understand why Union Carbide had been sold. He said, "I have worked long and hard to attain this position and I am the most qualified person to select this team." I am here to tell you that he did select the team and it was a disaster. The project ultimately succeeded, but there was a constant conflict between the owner's project manager and the contractor's project manager.

Back to the theme of practicing your profession: I had just joined BASF and been assigned to the Indigo Project. With just six weeks under my belt at the company, I was sent to headquarters in Germany to a meeting about the project. I had joined the company's New Jersey office six weeks earlier and had been the assigned project manager for five weeks. I arrived in Ludwigshaven, Germany, on Monday morning and went to the building I had been directed to, where they gave me a guide to show me around the plant. He took me to an enormous conference room--all in earth tones with high ceilings and no pictures on the walls--that held a table that could seat 30. He seated me in the middle of the table facing a wall of windows and left me alone.

I opened my briefcase and began setting out my presentation. Then, the German project manager came in and introduced himself. We had spoken over the phone but had never met in person. Soon, 26 more people filed into the room and sat down. Suddenly, the German project manager slammed his hand down on the table and said loudly enough for everyone to hear: "What qualifies you to be the project manager on this project?!?" I was glad to be wearing a suit so no one could see me sweating through my shirt!

Now, I know smoking is bad for you, but this time, it was very good for my mental health. I noticed that others were smoking in the meeting (it was still allowed in Germany at that time), so I took out a pack of cigarettes, slowly removed one from the pack and got out my lighter. I started "packing" the cigarette on the lighter, examining the cigarette after each hit on the lighter. Finally, I lit the cigarette and took a long drag. The whole process took about three minutes, during which the whole room was in complete silence. The German project manager was still standing directly across the table, waiting for an answer. During this whole time, while I appeared to be doing nothing but lighting a cigarette, my mind was racing to find an answer. Finally, after the drag on the cigarette, I gave him the only answer I could come up with: "Twelve years of working for a good German company, Rohm and Haas." There was silence for a moment, but then a tall grey-haired gentleman at the other end of the room said, "I think that is sufficient. Please proceed with your presentation." I later learned that this man was the director of engineering for BASF worldwide. This kind of calm approach to a delicate and politically charged situation can only be accomplished after you have practiced your profession.

This ability to recognize political situations becomes more acute during this time in your career. Have you ever watched a CEO fielding questions during an employee all hands? They often repeat the question before answering. Some may assume they want everyone to hear the question, but really they are giving themselves a moment to formulate an answer, giving everyone a sense of calm competence. This ability to remain calm in a storm is a hallmark of a great leader — and of a great project manager.

9: DEVELOPING YOUR PERSONA

As you develop into a mature project manager, you develop a persona and political habits that those who work with you have to deal with. Some are quiet and efficient; others are loud and boisterous. Most seek a reputation as fair and hard-working. But just because your persona is developed doesn't mean that you shouldn't examine it and decide if you are satisfied. Even if the building blocks are set, you can still change certain aspects of your political interactions.

I guess the best description of my persona at this point in my career can be best understood through a story. We were at the end of a very difficult project and the whole team gathered for a celebration. The electrical engineer and I didn't get along—so much so that he had asked to be removed from the project. He didn't like to be told to follow procedures and meet deadlines, but I handled it well and he stayed on the project. I had learned by this point to avoid politically charged situations when people were drinking, but it couldn't be avoided in this case. The electrical engineer had a drink in hand and asked for the floor. He said, "I still don't like you. I won't ever invite you to my house for dinner. But if you ever put another project team together, I would like to be on it." That was me: you didn't have to like me; you just had to respect me.

There were other political quirks I had developed. When I wanted someone to feel at ease—even if the situation was difficult—I would go to their office. This helped me control the situation in a relaxed atmosphere. But when I was truly upset and having a hard time with someone, I would ask them to come to my office, often after a waiting period (for instance, sending a message at 8 a.m. saying, "George, I'd like to see you in my office at 4 p.m."). A close friend and colleague told me that my team members were all aware of my political quirks, but I didn't mind.

Another few political skills that excellent project managers must hone are being a good listener—and being a good spear catcher. Listening doesn't need much explaining, but spear catching? This is a key ingredient and one that is honed in company politics. As a project manager, sometimes you have to yell at team members to motivate them or to help them understand their place in the team concept. You can gain a reputation as a tyrant, but it's important to be a benevolent dictator. When someone outside of the team throws a spear at one of your team members, you have to defend your team member, intercept the shot, and "catch the spear." As the leader, you have to take the blame, defend your team and correct the situation without fanfare.

This political perspective makes it clear that no one attacks any of the team members except the project manager. This will be deeply appreciated by your team and help you to be seen as a leader. You have to remember that, as you are gaining an understanding of the politics from above, you are also developing your own politics. Your management style is probably already formed, but now you are developing the delivery of your style. Just remember not to mimic the politics from above. Learn from what you see and try to make it a better place for aspiring young project managers.

10: LEARNING TO INSPIRE

In the last chapter, I talked about being a strong project manager, but that doesn't always make you well liked. So, how do you inspire your team while being strong?

As a young project manager at Rohm and Haas, we were sent to interpersonal skills training at Dixon House through Temple University. I especially recall one exercise where we were sent out of the room and the team was given a team personality — either laissez-faire, combative or cooperative. When you returned to the room, you had to recognize the team personality and direct them appropriately, accomplishing the goal of building something with tinker toys in 15 minutes. I came back and quickly went about directing the team, which I was certain was the "combative" team. I assigned each team member a part to build so I could keep them apart and stop them from arguing until I brought them together at the end. They followed my instructions well until about 5 minutes before the deadline. When I brought them back together, they reworked the model, ignoring my objections. I tried desperately to control them, failing miserably. It turned out that I had the cooperative team, not the combative one, so my management didn't work with them.

This provides a great lesson in managing a team. You

can't only be aware of your own political perspective; you have to really understand the politics of the team and its emotional make-up in order to inspire them. Shortly after the Indigo Project was cancelled at BASF, I was called into Rod's office for reassignment. I was asked to take over a new project that was going badly. The team had been put together quickly and all of the discipline leads were top flight—but they weren't working together and they weren't working well with the engineering design firm. Over the transition week, my assessment of the team was exactly the same as Rod's: they had talent and strong personalities, but no leader to inspire them.

Over my first few months, there were a number of incidents that shaped the attitude and direction of the team. The first incident occurred when I was called by the design firm's project manager to review a problem with me at the plastic scale model in the drafting room. Now, this design firm had a reputation as the IBM of the engineering world—all in suits and ties, no sport jackets. I arrived at the model in my three-piece suit and found the project manager with his entourage, including the civil engineer. About 35 others were there at their drafting tables, within earshot of this meeting.

The project manager began explaining the problem and the even bigger problems it would cause in the overall design. I began to realize that I had been ambushed. I was being led down a path of a lot of expensive extras, without my team around to provide their input. I asked the project manager to wait a moment while I took my jacket off and neatly folded it over a chair. I laid down on the floor, put my hands behind my head, looked up at the project manager and stated, "You may proceed."

The project manager had a startled look on his face and asked, "What are you doing?" I told him, "If I'm going to get screwed, I want to be lying down so I can enjoy it." The entire room broke into laughter. When it died down, the project manager said, "If you have the guts to do that, I'll just fix the problem and there won't be an extra." Needless to say, this got back to my team within hours.

The second incident involved the design engineering firm's formality. Braun policy was that everyone who used the cafeteria in the building had to wear proper attire (meaning they had to wear a jacket). Now, I had a brilliant process engineer on my team named Ralph, who showed up to work every day in corduroys and a flannel shirt with a tie that didn't match. He wore a ponytail and a full beard — very unusual for an engineer in the seventies. He was certainly unusual, but he was the brightest and hardest working process engineer I had ever met.

One Monday morning, a group from the design engineering firm came to my office, led by their project manager. They started off complaining about Ralph's appearance, but they were particularly offended that he ate at their "restaurant" without wearing a jacket. I listened politely for what felt like a very long time until they finally finished with, "What are you going to do about it?"

After a short pause, I restated their complaints,

pointing out that they really didn't object to Ralph's clothing; they objected to his existence. I also pointed out that their "restaurant" was really just an employee cafeteria and until they hired waitresses, it would remain a cafeteria. I informed them that not only would Ralph keep eating there without a jacket; from that point forward, the rest of my team would be eating there without jackets. From that point on, we did just that.

    The third incident involved the team's electrical engineer. The engineering design firm was in charge of buying equipment, reviewing vendor prints, and implementing the design. BASF's policy was for the discipline engineer (in this case, the electrical engineer) to review and approve the vendor prints, which would allow the design firm to move forward. This involved reviewing and stamping the prints and then forwarding them to me for signature. Well, this particular electrical engineer had a chip on his shoulder about this. He said that he wasn't going to sign anything because it was the design firm's job to get it right. He sent a small stack of prints to me without his signature. I sent them right back. We went round and round like this for several weeks, which was holding up the design and stopping other team members from moving forward with their work. Finally, the stack of prints needing approval had become very large. One Monday morning, I found the entire stack back on my desk. The engineer complied with the letter of my instruction by signing each page with a different signature — for instance, R. M. Nixon and Sid Vicious. I decided to call it a win, signed the drawings and passed them on to the design firm for processing. The team applauded my actions to get past this impasse and we became very close.

The point is, in order to inspire people, you have to understand what makes them tick — and what the politics of each particular team are. What I did worked for this team, but it might not have worked for another one. You have to develop your approach after fully understanding how the individuals are wired and how they work together.

11: LEARNING TO USE PEOPLE (BUT IN A NICE WAY)

"It's a thin line between Saturday night and Sunday morning."[2]
-Jimmy Buffett

The difference between using people in a nice way and just simply using them is often the difference between a successful career in project management and a career change. I have never understood people who promoted themselves using other people's efforts and thought they were successful. Truly successful managers inspire the people around them to do their best work and then give those people the credit. I learned early on that managers who produce high quality employees that everyone wants on their team are the best managers.

Engineers, as a type, tend to be frugal. This can work against a project manager who fails to understand that an inexpensive holiday gift or a token on Administrative Professionals Day can go a long way in the world of politics. It's the little things that can sway people and get them in your corner—bringing your assistant a cup of coffee, making the

---

[2] Jimmy Buffett, "Fruitcakes," 1994.

coffee if you're the first one in the office, making your own copies when it's convenient. If the copy room is backed up on your project, go offer to help. You'll find that they will work twice as hard for you as they will for someone else. Explaining to someone that you're in a bind and could use any help they could give goes a lot further than ordering someone to help you. It's this kind of stored up good will that you can really use if you can inspire it in people.

When I first took over as General Project Manager for Union Carbide, I realized I was going to need some help — and not the kind you can order up. Morale and pride were at an all-time low. I was coming in during a reorganization that included some layoffs, plus I was still considered an outsider and not part of the "Carbide family." During an engineering meeting, I noticed that one of the designers was very outspoken and seemed distrustful of me and of management in general. He was part of our Institute Plant and had a small office in a construction trailer. I decided to try to win him over. When I went to his office, I found that he didn't have a chair, so I turned over a trashcan and sat on it for two hours, hearing him out. He told me that this was the first time a General Project Manager had ever come to see him in his 20-plus years at the company. I visited him about once a week and I used him to leak new policies and gauge reaction. You could say that I used him, but we developed a mutual respect and became friends. I needed his access to people and information and he felt valued by the attention and influence he had because of our relationship. This is what I mean by using people — but in a nice way. Yes, I got what I needed, but I also developed this employee and achieved excellent results. And when the good people and projects start coming from your team, that gets noticed.

I remember one year when the Director of Engineering wanted everyone's offices to be sparkling clean. He assigned one of his direct reports (an associate director) to give everyone's offices a grade from 1 to 10 (with 1 being the worst) one Saturday morning. During the first inspection, I got a five, but so did my boss — so no big deal. I was focused on the work, not the cleanliness of my office. Unfortunately, during the next inspection, my boss's grade rose to an 8 and mine fell to a 2. I was told to clean my office. I didn't have time since I was working out of town — but that gave me a loophole. I had a modem connected to my computer and had to keep it on all the time, so I used this to convince the maintenance team that my office needed a lock (though none of the offices had locks at the time). With the lock on the door, the associate director couldn't get in to inspect my office — so I didn't get a grade. This went on for about six months. Then, one Wednesday morning, I got a call from an assistant (remember: getting those cups of coffee, making copies, remembering Administrative Professionals Day), telling me that the associate director got a key from maintenance and an inspection was coming on Saturday. I couldn't get there to clean my office, so on Friday, I told maintenance that I lost my key and they should change the lock to avoid a breach of my computer. So, when the AD came in on Saturday, his key didn't work. Needless to say, that assistant got a little bigger gift that holiday.

12: DEVELOPING TEAMWORK WITH AN ATTITUDE

If there's one thing I've learned over the years it's this: if it's not fun coming to work, find something else to do! Of course, in order to make the work fun, you have to really understand the politics. Once you do, you can make things fun or implement, "teamwork with an attitude."

Making things fun doesn't mean you have to be silly or arrogant. When I first got to Union Carbide, morale was terrible. People rarely laughed and hardly made eye contact when they passed in the hallway. It was a miserable place to work. Around this time, a young engineer named Stan transferred back into the department and noticed the lack of humor. We decided to lighten things up by joking around and greeting each other loudly with things like "Good morning, sweetheart!" in a sarcastic and silly manner.

During this time, I hired a temporary secretary. One morning, Stan and I came in at about the same time. We saw each other from opposite ends of the hallway and I called out, "Good morning, sweetheart!" and blew him a kiss. Right at that moment, the new temp stepped out of her office facing me and didn't see Stan at the other end of the hall. She turned beet red and ducked back into her office. She was shaken and told one of the other assistants about the incident. The other woman looked up casually and said, "Don't worry, that wasn't for you. The good morning kiss was for Stan." My new secretary did get over it and stayed on for several years, telling me later that she appreciated how I made things fun at work. Although this may just seem like antics, it made a big difference. The over-the-top greeting between Stan and I lightened things up and people started to laugh again. And eventually, other people started greeting each other in the mornings—but just in a friendly way.

Another story that comes to mind about injecting fun into work relates to that team of intelligent misfits that was always a work in progress. One of the things that the high class design firm did to destroy my team's morale was to issue parking tickets in their parking lot. You couldn't back into parking spaces because the exhaust would ruin the grass. Your tires couldn't touch the painted lines. It was ridiculous. Their maintenance team went around the parking lot every morning and every afternoon putting these irritating pieces of paper on everyone's windshields. This caused a lot of grumbling on the team. At the start of the new month, I put a note on the bulletin board: "The BASF engineer who receives the most tickets this month will receive a free lunch from the project manager (me)." My brilliant, eccentric process engineer won that month and actually held the record with 31 tickets in a 20 workday month! Needless to say, morale picked up tremendously.

I was lucky that the General Manager of the design firm, Bob, found my approach entertaining. He allowed me to continue with the contest. When the Director of Engineering for BASF came to lunch, Bob told him the story of me lying on the floor in the drafting room. After lunch, the director said he liked my style and asked if there was anything he could do to help me. I asked for his help with a tricky personnel problem and he helped me out (I'll tell you more about that later.)

The game I made out of the parking tickets didn't hurt anyone. In fact, it even helped with morale at the design firm. We started posting the results weekly and people started waiting around the bulletin board to find out who was in the lead. Having an understanding of the politics of the design firm's leader helped me to formulate the right plan. I could have just approached Bob and asked that his people stop giving my folks tickets. The approach I took was more fun for my team and created some fun for Bob's team, too. It went a long way to create a team with an attitude.

13: LEARNING TO BE A SPEARCATCHER

Being a good spearcatcher can be painful (no pun intended). As a project manager, you have to catch the spears when someone on your team is unaware of company politics — or just makes a mistake. Luckily, none of the mistakes I encountered in my three-plus decades were catastrophic. And in these situations, I found that honesty really helped to soften the blow.

I learned this lesson early, but it took a while to sink in. I was in charge of testing pipe on a project in Texas and I was running a little behind schedule. In order to make up the time, I skipped some steps. Instead of taking the control valves out of the line and replacing them with dummy valves for testing, I decided to run the test through several of the control valves. This might not have been so bad, but I didn't even check the pressure rating on the control valves. Needless to say, I ruined several valves, but fortunately, they were steel and stock items. Of course, this got back to the project manager. He called me into his office and I could see he was angry. Before he could say a word, I said, "I screwed up, but I'll fix it and make up the time somehow." He gave me a funny look and said, "I wish you hadn't said that. I was getting ready to chew you out, but now you made that hard to do."

Now that incident was a little uncomfortable, but

didn't cause any real pain. Spearcatching gets tougher when the problems are bigger, though. When I was General Project Manager at Union Carbide, I was told to work on a rush project to install a new boiler. I assigned an engineer to prepare the estimates and set up the team. Without seeking engineering input, the business team had submitted an appropriation request for $4 million. We objected, but no one listened and we were told to proceed. The project engineer brought it in on time, but it cost $4.7 million. This created quite a stir, because any project that was over by more than 10% had to be reauthorized, which had to be accompanied by a lengthy explanation. The business team was telling the vice president of engineering that it was his folks who screwed things up. As a result, he was pushing for the name of the person responsible.

Now, it's important to understand a bit about the culture of Union Carbide at the time. I remember one meeting I was in where a project manager said, "I truly thought you were going to fire me for what happened on this project." One of the engineering directors looked him in the eye and said, "Here at Carbide, we don't fire people for their mistakes. We keep you around so we can punish you for several years." I had seen multiple people who were carrying grudges against subordinates and couldn't even remember why they had been angry. So, this was the backdrop for this project overage.

It was pretty obvious that the heat was cascading downhill and heading in my direction. A letter from the VP of engineering to the director of project execution landed on my desk with a handwritten note: "Please respond ASAP." At this point, it would have been easy to sacrifice the project engineer. But my response was classic spearcatching. I responded that I was the person responsible because I had allowed an estimate to be submitted without engineering input. I also attached a copy of the e-mail from 18 months earlier complaining to the business folks about the estimate. I went on to explain that any further explanation would have to come from the business team, since they were solely responsible for the estimate. I saved my team, but the business made sure that I got the lowest ranking the next year and was blocked from getting a raise. When the director of project execution told me, my response left him speechless: "That's OK. You're already paying me more money than I ever thought I would make, and I'm having too much fun to worry about a small raise in pay."

Given the company policy of keeping people around to punish them, being a spearcatcher became an art form. After the boiler project, management decided to put in a second boiler and I assigned the same project engineer. This time, though, we were allowed to prepare the estimate and we brought it in on time and on budget. Now this project engineer had been with Carbide for more than twenty years and he was well aware of their punishment policy. When he got this second assignment and got his raise, he knew what I had done. He came to me after completing the second boiler project and said, "Because of what you did for me, I probably worked harder and put in longer hours on this project than on any project I worked on in the past twenty years." These are the kind of results you can expect from spearcatching.

Now, spearcatchers aren't always seen in a favorable light and there are two groups who see it this way. The first is management—but that can be corrected as more of you good project managers who are reading this book are promoted into management. This presupposes that you learn from your predecessors. I hope you'll keep this book around as a reminder to laugh and have fun.

The second group is tougher—and it's possible they may never get it. This is human resources. They used to be called personnel when they looked after the needs of employees, but it seems that more and more, their responsibility is to hand down policies from management, no matter how silly. I've met some good HR folks, but in general, they don't have a clue—and the best ones tend to be shipped far from headquarters. HR rarely understands leadership in an engineering environment and doesn't make much of an effort to learn. They treat any manager who becomes a spearcatcher as a threat to the management chain of command.

Before I retired, I did see a ray of hope. The vice president of engineering at Dow Chemical regularly practiced spearcatching and understood its value. I'm sure he was constantly at odds with HR.

14: STILL ALIVE AND READY TO MOVE ON

As I came to the end of my "parenting" phase, I not only felt secure in my technical knowledge, but also in who I was as a person. This change happened at the end of my first year as a General Project Manager for Union Carbide. Two things happened at the end of that year that made me realize I could deal with the politics of any corporation.

The first thing that happened was an in-depth performance review with my boss, the Director of Project Execution (gotta love that title!). In that review, we went over my year's performance against a set of goals. He spent three hours going through the details and discussing how well I had done in accomplishing those goals. Then, he spent the next hour explaining that I had not really accomplished the goal of becoming a Union Carbide manager. Here, in Chapter 14, I can honestly tell you that I did exactly what I've been warning you about: I ignored everything I had learned through experience and tried to be someone I wasn't. My boss explained that if I had another year like the one I just had, I would probably be demoted back to project manager (notice that he didn't say he would fire me). At that moment, I decided to become the GPM that I should have been based on my experience, not the one that Union Carbide thought I should be.

The second thing that happened related to the young, enthusiastic project manager with a master's in project management who had been assigned to my group. He came to me and said, "I'm not learning anything and my talents are being wasted." He was right. He'd been working in my group for eight months and I hadn't taught him anything. And from what I could gather, neither had anyone else. My goal had always been to become a mature adult who was a teaching project manager, but sometime in the course of one year, I had forgotten that.

After I let all of this sink in, I set a meeting with my boss—you know, the Director of Project Execution. At this point, I wasn't entirely aware of the "don't fire, simply punish forever" policy. I knew that I had to change and I knew that my organization had to change. I also knew that I needed some incentive to make it work—and my boss needed some incentive to help me accomplish this. I quickly went about assessing my staff and drafting up some much-needed changes. I also reviewed the workload and found a $12 million project coming up that had been unassigned. I penciled in my young friend's name and reassigned him to report directly to me.

When the day of my meeting with my boss arrived, I was extremely calm. I started out by telling him that he was absolutely correct. I said, "I have not lived up to expectations over the last year." Of course, I meant that I had not lived up to my own expectations—not his. I told him that I appreciated his evaluation and his candor about demoting me if I didn't improve. Then, I promised him that if I didn't improve by the next year, I would quit. This gave him the motivation that he needed to help me, regardless of his motives. The look on his face was priceless, especially since he didn't want me in this position and still felt I was an outsider.

I took advantage of the momentum by requesting the personnel changes I needed and he gladly agreed. We made small talk and discussed the schedule for the changes. I could sense that he was looking forward to going home and breaking out a bottle of celebratory wine. I left his office knowing that I had one year to prove that what I have written in this book could really work. I was also determined to prove that leadership is earned, not copied.

During the next year, I had the best numbers of all of the GPMs. Our morale was greatly improved and people were having fun at work. I got a favorable review and a raise (a small one). One of the individuals that I replaced was sent off to a foreign assignment after stating publicly that there was no way I could have him replaced because his 32 years with the company counted for something. Obviously, he didn't understand company politics. Once he was replaced, people stopped me in the halls and sent me e-mails saying, "It's about time."

Here's the takeaway: when you gain that confidence in your ability and you've learned how to use company politics to your benefit, you can affect change. You have to learn from your mistakes, and if you're still alive, move on and don't duplicate the mistakes of others. Once, I was asked what I wanted to be when I grew up. My answer at that time was "I don't know." Over the next several chapters, though, I will show you what I really wanted to be when I grew up: a teaching project manager with a sense of humor—one who loved what he did for a living and thought that work should always be fun!

15: UNDERSTANDING BIG BUSINESS POLITICS - VP AND ABOVE

In large, multinational corporations, the top echelon arrived at the top from hard work and successes in their fields. They also understood and worked the politics to their advantage. As a career project manager, you need to understand your area of the business. In fact, your career depends on it. Even if you think you are so far down the ladder that this won't affect you — believe me, it will. We are seeing a trend of companies moving to flatter organizational structures with larger span of control for managers. A prime example of this is Dow Chemical, who boasts that you are never more than six people removed from the president.

What this means is that you will come in contact with the vice presidents — whether of engineering or business groups — quite frequently. This chapter is about situations we encounter every day. Someone with more authority walks into your office and asks, "What do you think of this project?" Your natural instinct is to blurt out the truth. This approach has ruined many careers, or at least slowed them down. In that split second before answering, ask yourself: "Do I know how he or she feels about this project?" If you don't know the answer to this question, be very careful with your answer.

I had an interesting experience during my "mature years" that will illustrate that no matter how careful you are, there are things beyond your control. I had just been promoted to general project manager in January 1994 while I was still the project manager on a major ($60M) expansion project. The VP of the business group (who I got along with very well) decided to retire that very month. A new VP was announced who I didn't know — and I surely didn't know his politics. The project was nearing completion in early June when I was invited to play golf in the business group's annual outing. Of course, I accepted.

Now it's important to know that the project was running over budget by about 9%. With all of the information available to me, I felt confident that we would not exceed the 10% allowable overrun limit. In fact, it looked like we had an $800K cushion before we hit that limit.

Now, back to the golf outing. I called up the person who had sent me the invitation to find out about my foursome. That's when I learned that the VP of the business group had requested that I not only be in his foursome, but ride is his cart with him. I had two weeks to prepare, anticipating that he would ask whether reauthorization would be required. In those two weeks, I did everything possible to be sure I knew what the costs were. I checked all of the invoices, tax issues, shipping charges. I was sure I had everything covered and we were still $800K to the good.

The golf day arrived and I admit, I was nervous. I played poorly. The VP questioned me on all aspects of the project after every shot. Finally, on the 16th hole, he asked me the dreaded question about reauthorization. For two holes, I gave him every noncommittal answer I could think of. Finally, on the 18th hole, he asked me for a yes or no answer. I rushed right in with a firm, "No reauthorization will be necessary." He thanked me and suggested I take some golf lessons. Then he invited me into the bar for a drink and (as he put it) "no more talk about business."

In the next two weeks, our accounting department informed me that they had found a lost invoice for $1M that wasn't part of any forecast. This meant reauthorization and I had to inform the VP. Needless to say, the punishment began immediately and forgiveness took about a year. As I mentioned before, I erred more than I succeeded — but I'm trying to help you, young project manager, to avoid some of my mistakes.

Let me tell you about another incident that looked like a roadmap for disaster. We have all had one or two of these projects. The project was approved with an "appropriation grade" estimate (+/- 10%), but that estimate was terribly flawed, as it was put together by someone who had no real knowledge of either this kind of project or project management in general. After about two months of work to scope and prepare for this project, it became very clear that the actual cost would likely be double the initial estimate. Unfortunately, there was no data in the original estimate, so it was difficult to run a comparison. As I was dealing with this dilemma and feeling very frustrated, the director of engineering entered my office accompanied by the vice president of the business group and the VP asked, "What do you think of this project?" At this point in my career, I had learned a little about politics, so I took a moment to consider the situation. I was very certain the director of engineering hadn't put this estimate together and I couldn't imagine it was the VP of the business group, so I answered: "Whoever put this estimate together should be fired." I went on to detail how difficult it would be to justify the huge increase, since the initial estimate was so flawed.

A strange silence ensued and I began to feel I had just ridden into the Valley of Death. Finally, the VP spoke: "I put that estimate together." He turned and left my office with the director of engineering in hot pursuit. The next day, I was abruptly reassigned. The announcement stated that the project I was reassigned to was very important and they need my expertise. They also named my replacement. I was lucky; the director of engineering saved me. But I was never assigned to another project for that business group until after that VP retired.

The bottom line is that politics exist at every level in large organizations. Do your research before you speak. If you're not sure, be as noncommittal as possible. For those new to the game, I'm sorry to have to acquaint you with this. But it's also a reminder for those who have been at it a while. Hopefully, you can master the art of politics in project management before you are forty and not have to wait until you are ready to retire!

16: PREPARING YOUR TEAM, *OR* CAUTIOUS REALISM

Once you've learned to avoid the political landmines, it's time to move on to the next step. And no, I don't mean quitting! Project managers do not work alone—they lead project teams. As the project manager, you are the leader of an orchestra, full of musicians, each of whom belongs to a different union.

When you present to senior leadership, you're likely to have one or more members of your team with you. This means that they also need to understand the politics. Here comes the part you may not like: it's your job to train your team to handle every situation. If one of them slips up, you have to take responsibility (remember that chapter on being a spearcatcher?).

In fact, the project I mentioned in that spearcatching chapter about the project cost overrun has an interesting lesson here. If you recall, that project had been estimated (by the business) at $4M and was authorized by the Board for +/- 10% even before engineering knew about the project. So, bring the project in for $4.4M or less and you're a hero. Bring it in for even a dollar more and you have a lot of explaining to do, plus you have to put together a reauthorization package. While this project was going on, I was very busy on several other projects (you know the corporate initiative: do more with less), and I had been traveling a lot to another jobsite, so I turned the project over to one of our more experienced project engineers.

In order to protect the guilty and punish the innocent, let's call him Sam. I knew that Sam had been passed over for project manager due to his caustic attitude toward upper management. He had encountered company politics and been clobbered by them. Sam finished the project, had a very successful startup and turned in his final report with all of the cost data. The project completed for $4.7M. This meant a meeting with the business VP and reauthorization.

I asked Sam to come along, since I was the project manager of record and he had all of the details. I took great pains to warn Sam about the politics of dealing with this particular VP and his zeal for ruining project managers' careers. I explained it to Sam like this: just answer any factual questions and leave the loaded ones to me. The meeting proceeded well because the project had met its schedule and it had a very good startup. Sam did well. He behaved himself and followed my instructions to the letter.

At the end of the meeting, the VP looked over at Sam and said, "Can you have the revised appropriation request ready in three days?" What happened next went so fast that I didn't have a chance to stop it. Sam blurted out, "You are going to pay the extra $300K. What's the big hurry getting the paperwork done?" The silence was deafening. I jumped in and said, "We will certainly have the paperwork done in three days or less." The VP's reply was, "This meeting is over. Mr. Davis, I want to see you in my office immediately."

When the two of us were alone in his office, the VP did his best to crucify Sam, but I stepped in and caught the spear, explaining that I had failed to properly train Sam. Then, the VP did his best to crucify me. After telling me how he would punish me, he asked if I had anything to say. Calmly, I explained that his star business manager had prepared the estimate. He jumped in and said that I had approved it. This was when I produced a year-old email from his business manager stating that he had prepared the estimate and that it had already been approved. My reply was attached, where I noted that the estimate was too low but that we would make every effort to bring it in for the authorized amount. The crucifixion was over and this was a fine example of a political battle waged and thwarted. Sam went on to complete the second project under budget with a beautiful startup.

During the course of most projects, project teams are called upon to make presentations to visiting dignitaries. This can range from the business leader to the president of the company. As the leader, you have to learn as much about the audience as possible. Use whatever resources you can to find out what that person wants to hear. Once you have that information, give the team their "do's"
and "don't"s for the meeting.

As the project manager on one of those high profile projects, I had a visit from the director of engineering one day. During the meeting, he told me that the VP of manufacturing for the plant where we were building the project wanted a review meeting. The meeting was set for two weeks out. The team was working very hard, as we were only in the first third of the project. Still, the director told us to stop what we were doing and spend the next 3-4 days preparing slides and holding review meetings. The presentation changed constantly and we were informed of the VP's reputation for slamming engineering and ruining project team morale.

On the fifth day, I finally called the VP without informing the Director. I asked about his itinerary, how long he expected to spend with us, and what he wanted to discuss. Much to my surprise, he answered the phone and we had a good conversation about the project. At the end of the conversation, he thanked me and said he wished that other project managers would do the same, as this would save us all a lot of time. I revised the agenda and told the Director what I had done. The meeting went well, the VP was pleased and the Director was pleased. The project team got high praise for their knowledge of the project and the wonderful presentation they had done. All of this was a result of the fact that my assistant had called his assistant to find out how a phone call from me would be received.

There are many ways to avoid tricky political situations, but there are also too many traps out there to avoid them all. One of the things that prompted me to write this book was my curiosity about why the subject is never talked about or taught at the college level. I once asked a seasoned project manager (who doesn't seem so old to me now) why the subject was always avoided. He claimed that, first of all, no company wants to admit that politics exist. And if you don't talk about it, it isn't there. A second, everyone goes through it, so people think that everyone coming up through the ranks should endure the same torture.

One night at a dinner, I was seated next to a VP and asked him the same question. His reply may shock you: "Politics were forced on me when I was coming up through the ranks and now it's my privilege to force it on the people who work for me now." Cautious realism occurs when I remember a quote in Colin Powell's *A Leadership Primer*. He said that sometimes "being responsible means pissing people off." I always remember this when it comes to politics and realize my goal and yours will be to minimize and soften the blows.

17: DOING IT YOUR WAY

So many people end up in project management by accident, but eventually, some realize that they want to be project managers for the rest of their lives. That's when it starts to get fun! When you get up in the morning and look forward to the challenges the day will bring, you have arrived at your chosen profession. This doesn't mean you have to give up on your ambition of being a vice president of engineering, but you might be happy running project engineering. This is a nice place to be if you don't mind teaching young engineers and haven't forgotten what a spear catcher is supposed to do. Remember (another Colin Powell lesson): the day people working for you stop bringing you their problems is the day you have stopped leading them. If enough people in positions of authority read this book, we may end up being able to minimize politics in the engineering workplace.

OK, so let's get to the title of this chapter: "doing it your way" (and I might add mischievously – getting away with it). Mr. Donald Ney was one of the very best at this. He once asked me, "Do you know what company standards are for?" I gave the normal response about uniformity of design, setting rules, utilizing best practices, etcetera. He was drinking a martini at the time. He set down his drink, looked at me and said, "Company standards and rules are there for really good project managers to use when they want to slow down a project—and when they want to speed up a project, they are there to tell you how to get around the problem." He also said that a project manager has to fully understand company rules and standards in order to apply this principle.

Some companies have job descriptions for project managers—how quaint! Shortly after I was hired at Union Carbide, I was getting overwhelmed by all of the rules and standards. But I also found it strange that a company with so many rules and standards didn't have a job description for project managers. The director of engineering named Maher Mansour and he was (and still is) one of the4 nicest men you would ever want to meet. He spent many years catching spears for me. He also worked hard to make me into a gentler person. He thought that everyone should love project managers.

Maher was hired a year before I came on board. He was always working late—until 7 or 8 pm. One evening, I walked into his office and asked, "Is there a job description for project managers in this company?" He said no and that he was sure of it because he had looked for one before he hired me. I responded, "Oh, that's great" and got up to leave. He asked me why and I told him that without the constraints of a job description, I was free to run my project however I wanted. He was taken aback by this, but after some discussion, he agreed. I must add here that bending the rules will sometimes bring unwanted attention to your project, but again, I would quote Colin Powell: "You don't know what you can get away with until you try."³

While I was at Union Carbide, I often used the expression, "Gee, I didn't know I wasn't allowed to do that. I'm new here." Finally, after about 5½ years, one of my bosses said, "Roy, you're not new here anymore. Please lose that line."

Of course, I didn't just come up with this habit of "doing it my way" at Union Carbide. Earlier in my career, when I worked for BASF, I was on a project that was moving to the field. All of the contracts had been awarded, which required eight signatures (and about a month of time). We had multiple lump sum contracts for each of the disciplines, including a $15,000 contract for general site work like setting up the trailers, hooking up the temporary electric service and other items. As we got underway, I realized that this was a union job and there were a number of things missing from the contracts. For instance, the union rule stated that, if you have more than eight welding machines on the job site, you have to hire an operating engineer (who often tends to be the brother-in-law of the business agent or something like that). Each of the discipline contractors made sure they did not exceed eight machines, but the combined total was well over eight. Since we were the general contractor, it fell to us to hire that operating engineer.

This was only one of a number of things that surfaced

---

³ Powell, Colin. "A Leadership Primer." United States Department of the Army, 2006.

and made me realize that I needed to write and issue a new contract. Unfortunately, that process might take two months and we didn't have that kind of time. Since I knew BASF's rules well, I realized that I could use the general site contract and write field change orders. Their rule on this was that a project manager could authorize up to $15,000 without any approval, but it did not specify any limit on the number of times this could happen or the percentage of the original contract that it could make up. So, this $15,000 original site contract became my catch-all contract and I managed to turn it into a $150,000 contract through field change orders--$15,000 at a time.

Fortunately, this was a very successful project and a very successful startup. During the final review of costs, however, the auditors noticed the large increase to this small contract. I was called into a big meeting with purchasing and accounting to explain myself. I did explain and I pointed out that I had not violated any rules. Finally and reluctantly, they agreed. Of course, they quickly changed the rules to close this loophole.

The key takeaway from this chapter is that you have to use both your knowledge of politics and of company rules, plus your experience, if you want to "do it your way." Always remember the expression, "it's easier to beg forgiveness than ask for permission." Good project managers don't wait for an official blessing to try something new. They are prudent and never reckless, but this lets them get away with saying, "sorry, I didn't know I wasn't allowed to do that." This only works if you have a good handle on the politics and you understand what will work. Something that every good project manager knows, though, is that if you ask enough people for permission, you will eventually find someone who believes it is their job to say "no."

If you want to slow your project down, ask permission. If you want to move forward prudently with a good idea, don't ask permission—just make sure it's within the rules. Look around at some of the least effective project managers. They almost always ascribe to the philosophy, "If I haven't explicitly been told yes, I can't do it." You will also notice that many of the most effective ones practice the philosophy, "If I haven't been told no, I can."

There is a world of difference between mediocrity and excellence, so step up to the plate and take a chance on excellence.

18: EXPERT WITH AN ATTITUDE

There is a saying that if you have to tell people you're in charge, you aren't really in charge. I have taken over teams at the beginning of a project who wanted to have me replaced but these same teams would take me out to dinner at the end of the project. I never had to tell anyone on a team who was in charge.

I'm reminded of another BASF project (when it was still Wyandotte Chemical) where I was working with someone who was an excellent engineer but lacked the interpersonal skills to be a really good project manager. During the design stage of the project, I was constantly working to heal the wounds he inflicted on the rest of the team. This engineer had many friends in high places and I knew it. When I sent him to the field to gather data, he always came back with everything completed, but I soon learned that the contractors called him "Mr. Clean Shoes" because of the way he went about it.

At one point, the contractor was attempting to fit up a large steel water pipe by heating the elbow, which was a very commonplace practice. My engineer saw this going on and stopped the job. He started quoting chapter and verse from the piping standards and also the handbook on pipe stress. I overheard the conversation and quietly told the contractor to continue what he was doing and put some paint on the heat marks as quickly as possible. I brought the project engineer into my field office and explained that this was a very common practice in the field and was acceptable on water piping.

A month before the end of the project, I had a call from the VP of one of the other operating divisions requesting that I release this engineer so he could become the project manager on a major expansion he was planning. I set up a lunch with the VP in order to "discuss the timing of the transfer." During that lunch, the conversation turned to my engineer and his qualifications and performance on my project. After listening for a while, the VP finally asked me whether I would put him in charge if this were my project. I answered with a definite "no." He asked me for a recommendation, which I gave him.

The next day, the project was announced and the person I had recommended was named project manager. It took my engineer about two weeks to learn about my lunch and recommendation. On the day he learned about this, we had a dinner planned with our spouses. While we were waiting for our table, the engineer began drinking and he kept it up during dinner. Finally, during coffee and dessert, he demanded in front of everyone that I tell him why I didn't recommend him for the assignment. I quickly suggested that we drop the subject and continue the conversation in my office on Monday. (Of course, if he had read the first few chapters of this book, he would have known not to talk business while drinking!)

The engineer persisted and finally, I raised my hand

and the group got quiet. I proceeded to tell my engineer that his behavior at dinner was typical of his behavior at work (without the alcohol) and that if he couldn't understand the out I was giving him to discuss it on Monday, he certainly wasn't capable of managing a project. There was silence and then, much to my surprise, my process engineer piped up: "I think he has you there!" The whole team clapped. Rich left quickly, but he did come to my office on Monday to apologize.

Understanding company politics has never been more important than it is today. Companies don't have loyalty to their employees anymore and employees don't feel loyalty to their companies. Given the frequent movement of employees between companies, it is critical to gain an understanding of company politics as quickly as possible.

When I first got promoted to general project manager at Union Carbide, my second in command was announced at the same time. As I mentioned before, he felt that my promotion should have been his. He resented me as an outsider and made no effort to hide it. He had friends in high places and my immediate boss had put him in his position as a favor, not because of his abilities.

Unfortunately, one of the easiest ways to demotivate talented people is to make them put up with people who have gotten where they are through political favors that don't match their work. We went through a downsizing and my whole group wondered why he was in a position of authority instead of laid off. The most creative and productive people we had came to me and asked why I wasn't dealing with this obvious problem. I asked them to be patient.

This guy had a habit of countermanding my directives and openly told the group not to worry because I wouldn't be around very long. I documented every incident and had people sign statements that they had been present when he did these things. Then, he crossed the last line. He told a very talented female project manager that she should be at home taking care of her kids instead of taking a job away from a man. He said the same to a clerk.

Finally, I saw my opportunity. My boss asked me to supply a project manager for a project in Kuwait. I didn't hesitate to nominate my problem employee. My boss objected, wondering why I wanted to get rid of him. That's when I produced all of my documentation, including the harassment complaints that I was preparing to take forward to HR. After reviewing my documentation, my boss informed him that he would be heading to Kuwait. His response was "I won't go. I have 32 years with this company." He wanted to have a meeting with my boss.

About an hour later, I was called into my boss's office where my second in command was waiting patiently for his reprieve. My boss invited me in and let me know that they were waiting for me to discuss the situation. Then, my boss said, "I'm going to read a list of things that occurred over the past year and I need you to either confirm or deny them." After hearing the list, his response was, "They're all true. What difference does that make?" My boss replied, "You will leave for Kuwait on Friday or I will have you fired for cause and you will lose your pension. Do you understand?" My group was happy because this problem had been removed and I was able to navigate around his relationships with the senior leaders. This is a prime example of using company politics to my advantage.

    The takeaway is that once you have learned the politics, you can use them to your advantage. Still, you can't advertise this expertise. People will notice how well you handle political issues when they come up and that will give you confidence. That's what everyone will notice.

19: CHOOSE YOUR ASSIGNMENTS

One day when I was sitting with my good friend Stan having a beer, I asked him the same question that had been asked of me — what he wanted to be when he grew up. I wasn't surprised when he said he didn't know, but I was a little surprised at his further clarification. Stan was 45 years old and had only worked at Union Carbide.

I explained that I had always wanted to be a director of project management or a director of construction and I had accomplished my goal. When I finally realized what I wanted to be, I researched the position, determined which experiences I would need to get there, and set about to have those experiences. Then, I asked Stan how he chose what jobs he accepted and turned down. He didn't seem to understand the question.

This is where it gets amazing. Stan said that when his boss called him in and told him what his next assignment would be, he just accepted it. He continued with (brace yourselves): "The company and its management will surely look out for me and my career. I've been with them since college." We concluded our discussion and our drinks without any further comment. But I'm here to tell you that if you want to be a professional project manager (or any other position for that matter), plot your own course. Set a goal and stick with it.

Company career planning sessions are gone. It's up to you to look out for yourself.

The difficult part is that sometimes, achieving your goal means moving on. Keep your resume and LinkedIn profile up to date. Also, be active in organizations like the Project Management Institute (PMI) and the Construction Industry Institute (CII). Being an active member means more than just paying your dues; it means getting involved. PMI has a certification program and they accept papers to be presented at their national convention. CII is made up of member companies, and if your company is a member, I encourage you to participate. It may require some of your newfound knowledge of company politics to be elected as the representative for your company. CII sponsors yearly practical research projects that are excellent. If you are fortunate enough to get on one of these teams, you will find it very rewarding. And most importantly, both of these organizations are great for networking with other members.

It was at one of these meetings when I made a significant career move. I was presenting at a PMI national convention and at one of the evening functions, I was approached by someone from BASF. He offered to set up an interview for me as a project manager and this was at a time when I was trying to get back into project management at Rohm and Haas. He told me that they had just purchased Wyandotte Chemical and were setting up their headquarters in Parsippany NJ. I agreed and that took me on to the next step of my career.

No matter where you are in calendar years, if you learn to master the world of corporate politics, you will have an opportunity to pick and choose your assignments. Learning to turn down a project in a way that makes the executive feel that it is the right decision is an art.

The last position I held at Union Carbide actually came out of an artful refusal. I was the general project manager for the West Virginia operations and was doing quite well. I had a whole year without a recordable injury and engineering was being done for 16-18% of TIC (total installed costs). I was having a great time and helping to train engineers both young and old. I was comfortable where I was in my career and I was in my early sixties with a lot of enthusiasm left for the job. What happened next shocked me.

My boss called me into a meeting and told me that I had been selected to be director of construction for all of Union Carbide. Now the bad news: management felt I could best serve the organization by relocating to Houston, TX. They needed an answer by the end of the week. Nothing against Houston, but I didn't want to move. I was comfortable where I was. I checked my sources and verified that, yes, the VP of engineering really wanted his director of construction in Houston.

I formulated a plan. I used the high cost of relocation and my age as a cornerstone for my refusal. I knew that the director would still have to fly out of Houston since there was only one plant there, and this factored into my calculation. I turned the job down because it seemed unlikely that the company could recoup the costs of my relocation before I retired. I strongly suggested that they find a local candidate in Houston.

The answer that came back was that, yes, I was absolutely correct on the relocation costs. But since the director would be flying to various locations anyway, they were willing to eliminate the relocation and allow me to use West Virginia as my base of operations. I had no recourse but to accept the position.

The lesson learned here is that you have to have a goal in your professional life. Chart your own course toward that goal. Many engineers have been sidetracked into doing something they didn't enjoy or got pigeonholed due to silly corporate politics. No matter where you are in your career, you can't lose sight of your goal. Learn the corporate politics and work them without inflicting them on others. Organizations don't really accomplish anything. Plans don't accomplish anything. Management theories don't accomplish anything. People do! Goals are achieved or missed because the people involved make it happen. If you attract the best people, you will accomplish your goal and have fun doing it.

20: CONCLUSIONS AND OTHER THOUGHTS

This is the most difficult part to write, because you all know by now that politics and project management don't mix. You also know that company politics exist—it's part of your professional life and a big part of shaping your future. Large, multinational companies that will succeed in the future will try to minimize company politics. When they are really bad, company politics can lead to the demise of the company. In any case, they cost a lot of money, especially when they stop people from telling the emperor that he has no clothes and it's not a pretty sight.

I have seen several examples of this kind of politics that are atypical, and they may have been a factor in the demise of the company where they took place.

The first example took place when I was working on a project that required the design, procurement and installation of several pieces of equipment. This company had a technology group that developed the design drawings, reviewed the vendor prints, and gave their stamp of approval on all equipment items. Their lead was smart, and was on the ASME Code executive committee, but he was getting on in years and wasn't doing it particularly gracefully. He had a habit of lecturing and when I first met him, he went on for an hour about how project managers with chemical engineering degrees just didn't get it before I finally got a word in edgewise to let him know my degree was in mechanical engineering.

So, I sent all of my pressure vessel equipment to his group for design. I did not send him a piece of equipment called a plate and frame filter press, though, since it is not a pressure vessel even though it operates above 15 psig. (A pressure vessel is a device that squeezes the fluid out of a slurry to produce a cake material.) I ordered the equipment and reviewed the vendor drawings without including the technologist. After approving the design, I asked our inspection group to go to the shop and set up an inspection schedule before shipment.

Since the inspection group reported to the technologist, he got wind of this. He called and requested a meeting to discuss "an urgent matter" and I agreed to meet the next day. In this meeting, he told me that I had to get a code stamp on any vessel operating above 15 psig in order to be in strict compliance with ASME code. This meant I had to get the code stamp on my filter presses. I let him know that the state where the vessels were being installed hadn't adopted ASME code, but we had upgraded most of our process vessels with code stamps for safety reasons. He left my office very upset.

A few days later, I was summoned to the Director of Engineering's office. He told me to get a quote on obtaining code stamps on these presses. When I tried to explain that this was not an ASME code state, he stopped me and said that OSHA required it. That was a new twist! I asked the vendor for the pricing and they told me it would take several weeks to get the pricing because they had never done this before. "How fortunate!" I thought. Now, I could send a letter to the local OSHA office explaining the process and the equipment and asking for a ruling on whether I needed the code stamp. Within a few days I heard from the local office. They said they couldn't make a ruling and they were forwarding my request to the district office in Philadelphia.

Their letter telling me that there was no need for a code stamp (and referencing the chapter and paragraph of their code that covered the ruling) arrived the very same day as the quote from the vendor, telling me that it would cost an additional $170,000 to get the code stamps. Armed with this information, I called a meeting with the technologist to let him know that I did not plan to waste $170,000 on unnecessary code stamps. The next day, I was again summoned to the Director's office. When I arrived, I found that the technologist was already there. The Director informed me that I had to obtain the code stamps and unless I had further questions, the meeting was over.

We all got up to leave, but as I was heading for the door, the Director asked me to stay for a few moments longer. He closed the door and told me that I was right about the code stamps, but the technologist had many friends in high places. Now, they had all been contacted about my actions and many of those friends had called the Director to complain. This was politics in the extreme.

A few days later, I received a letter from a corporate

lawyer letting me know that it was his job to contact OSHA for rulings, not mine. In the future, I was to contact him for help instead of doing things on my own. He also stated that a letter of reprimand was being placed in my personnel file for violating company policy.

In the end, the vendor failed to make the test and additional engineering costs were incurred to correct the problem. Plus, additional technologists had to be brought in. The total cost for the two code stamps ended up being $300,000. Needless to say, it all worked out well for the technologist and now this plant has the only two filter presses in North America with code stamps. What a huge waste of time and money over nothing but one man's ego and toxic company politics!

The second issue was on a much larger scale and really didn't involve engineering. This one was about a revised accounting system that brought the corporation to a complete standstill because no one could tell the emperor that he was naked.

The president of the company hired someone to come in and revamp an antiquated accounting system. He chose a system that was good for financial organizations and banking institutions, but had a shaky record in the chemical industry. The new system was highly accurate and precise, but extremely inflexible. The entire corporation was going to migrate onto this system and engineering would be the pilot department with the first implementation.

Because we were the first to try the system, we were

also the first to find its limitations. Unfortunately, no one spoke up to question the decision because everyone knew the president was behind the project. The company spent a great deal of money and effort to implement the system. Once everyone was trained and the phases were cut in, the old system was shut down. As everyone struggled with this system, those who spoke up publicly were demoted, transferred and generally treated badly since they were "not team players." Unfortunately, the president believed the marketing on the system and just wouldn't hear anything that contradicted it.

    The final blow came when the system was implemented in the operating plants. An order was placed for 4,000 pounds of product and it was entered into the system for shipping papers and invoicing. The trucks would we weighed and the total amount that had to be accounted for was 4,050 pounds. This was entered into the order but because the system was so inflexible, no one could figure out how to adjust the system to account for this. All shipments from the plant either stopped completely or were delayed to the point that customers became irate. A team was assembled to fix the invoices manually and get the shipments back on schedule, but the whole problem took about six weeks and close to one hundred people to correct.

    In the end, the vice president of IT quit and his second-in-command was fired. This mistake cost the company millions of dollars and untold harm to the company's relationships with customers—all due to company politics and nothing else.

Take these two examples to heart. This is what politics can do to careers, company reputations and our perception of the truth. I don't fool myself to believe that everyone reading this book will be able to reverse the politics in their organizations and replace them with straightforward truth and understanding. My only hope is that young project managers, engineers and executives in any type of company will be armed with knowledge of the devastating potential of politics and a few tips on how to mitigate them. I sincerely believe that an educated generation can change the future by railing against politics and doing the right thing for the customer and the company. I think about the impact that *Up the Organization* had on my professional life — and I hope that my book will do the same for you.

Let me leave you with one thought: You need to like going to work in the morning. Work should be fun — and if you can shift politics in your favor, it can be absolutely hysterical.

ABOUT THE AUTHOR

Roy Davis is a career project manager and mechanical engineer by training. He spent his career managing large-scale construction projects, primarily in the chemical industry and worked for the chemical giants, Rohm & Haas, BASF, Union Carbide and Dow Chemical. He holds a bachelor's degree from Drexel University and participated in post-baccalaureate training at Renssalaer Polytechnic Institute. During his long career, Mr. Davis prided himself on mentoring the next generation of project managers and was an active member and occasional speaker with the Project Management Institute and Construction Management Association of America. He is now retired and lives in Charleston, West Virginia, with this wife, Carolyn.

www.ingramcontent.com/pod-product-compliance
Lightning Source LLC
Chambersburg PA
CBHW022109170526
45157CB00004B/1553